SYNTHESIS

by

Torkom Saraydarian

T.S.G. Publishing Foundation, Inc.
Complete Line of Torkom Saraydarian's Works
P.O. Box 7068, Cave Creek, AZ 85327 USA
Tel: 480-502-1909 * Fax: 480-502-0713
www.tsgfoundation.org

Synthesis
ISBN10: 0-911794-18-2
ISBN13: 978-0-911794-18-2

Printed in the United States of America
Typography by A.E.G., Agoura
Printing by J.C. Graphics, Los Angeles

SYNTHESIS

"Only the rainbow of synthesis can bestow advancement."
AUM, para.497.

The keynote of the Aquarian Age is synthesis. Every age has its own keynote which is given by the constellation into which the Sun apparently enters and travels for approximately 2500 years. Those life forms which cannot assimilate the energy that radiates from the constellation or which cannot live according to the keynote slowly disappear from the Earth.

The new energy is the energy of synthesis, and as it increases its influence upon the Earth it brings in three very interesting results:

1. This energy stimulates the will aspect of any living form. If the living form, or human being is full of weeds, or full of maya, glamor and illusion, the energy will stimulate them and lead them to form certain groupings which are separative, aggressive and totalitarian. Through such groupings crime increases, separative politics gain power, and in all seven fields of human endeavor people create hindrances and obstacles against unification and synthesis. But this does not mean that this formation lasts. This is a phase, and the method used by Nature is to stimulate, expose and then annihilate obstacles through the power of synthesis.

2. The second result will be the increase of insanity, mental and emotional disorders and the appearance of lower psychism. When powerful energies pour into the planet and people are not ready to receive them, the energies exercise a great pressure upon their etheric centers, which are affected directly.

We see a great amount of mental diseases at this time, resulting in crimes. Also, we see the increase of lower psychism. Mediums are growing like mushrooms and misleading people with dire consequences.

3. The third result is that those people who are pure and exercise lofty thinking, charged with pure motive, will develop the precious sense of synthesis. Such people will be leaders of the incoming Sixth Race. They will demonstrate psychic energy, wisdom, joy and health, and will evoke trust and confidence.

A pure mind is a mind which does not carry or produce criminal, separative or destructive thoughts, or thoughts that are based on lies, illusion and vanity.

The energy of synthesis will radiate out from the beings of those who have a healthy body, clean emotions, organized and pure thoughts, and a drive to serve humanity. Such people will be so magnetic that they will exercise a great, enlightening and transforming influence upon multitudes.

The energy of synthesis brings with it the Divine Will into our life. It is not too easy to define the Divine Will, but we can state that the Divine Will is an urge which directs you toward right human relationship. It is simply goodwill, inclusiveness, tolerance, and righteousness. The Divine Will makes you see that in every human being there exists only the One Self, which must be brought into actualization.

The energy of synthesis expands your consciousness and evokes the values and virtues latent in others. Thus you become an agent of progress and unfoldment.

The energy of synthesis sees that a power is active behind all phenomena, events and happenings, trying to bring beauty out of chaos.

In synthesis one passes through a phase which people call by many names: renouncement, detachment, leaving the lower self behind, and the like. The idea is that there comes a time when one merges with the whole and "loses himself, to find himself." This is explained in the story of shaped stones.

One day a stonecutter shaped lots of stones and left them on the ground. The builder came and told the stones that it was the time to give up their freedom to be part of a huge temple. Some of them looked at themselves and thought, "Well, we are so beautiful, shaped, refined and cut. Why should we renounce our freedom and give up our

6

personalities to be a part of a great whole in which no one as an individual is recognized, but only the temple?"

The stones had long discussions. After a while one of them said, "Brothers, first of all, we must know that the reason we exist is not to be by ourselves but to be a part of a great building. It is true that we will lose our separate existence, but we will exist as the temple. Each one of us will be the temple, and we will stand for that for which the temple stands. We will present the idea, the vision, the beauty behind the temple. If I am serving the purpose of my existence in losing my separate self, I will do so gladly."

Saying this, the stone jumped into the hands of the builder and became the first cornerstone. The others silently followed him, and the temple was erected in a few months. Each stone tremendously enjoyed the melodies, the hymns and words spoken in the temple; and they advanced in their consciousness to be ready to pass from the mineral kingdom to the vegetable kingdom. Thus through their sacrifice they created a synthesis.

The first step of synthesis is to be shaped, to become sacred. The second step is to lose your lower self and give it for something higher. And that higher something is your higher Self, the more inclusive Self. You are only renouncing your limitation; you are sacrificing your hindrances on the path of synthesis.

The power of synthesis develops when the human consciousness transcends the mental plane and functions in the intuitional light. This is done through meditation.

Scientific meditation is a step-by-step withdrawal from mental levels and entrance into the Intuitional Plane. This is the goal of the New Age. Mental development must allow the human soul to function in the Intuitional Plane. It is on the Intuitional Plane that all jigsaw puzzles come together to form the completed picture. The completed picture is synthesis.

Synthesis is like a building process. The engineer comes and invites five people and says to them, "We are going to build a big temple.

"You go and build 20 doors exactly in this shape and size, with such-and-such handles, wood and colors.

7

"You go and prepare 20 windows. Here is the description.
"You prepare curtains with this description.
"You build a foundation.
"You build the rooms in this size.
"You prepare the plumbing.
"You prepare the electrical wiring."

All these people go and work and toil to do their individual task as perfectly as possible; but none of them knows exactly what the temple will look like. When everyone does his job, eventually the parts will come together and the temple will appear in its completed beauty. This is what synthesis is.

In synthesis you have the blueprint. The workers each work on one aspect of the blueprint. There is the phase of assembling and finishing.

The engineer is the one who functions on the Intuitional Plane, and he has the blueprint, which is an idea. Laborers or specialists are the mental faculties, which carry on specialized work.

The mind must prepare all parts perfectly. This is why the mind must not only be highly educated, but also creative and specialized in a certain direction.

After the mind does its job, the human soul, the owner of the temple, synthesizes all that is done for the temple. Synthesis starts from the moment when the human soul sees the inner relationship between the completed parts in the light of the blueprint.

The process of synthesis never ends. After the temple is built, the temple becomes a part of a city; the city becomes a part of a country; the country becomes a part of a continent, and so on...until one realizes that all that he was doing was preparing elements to build the Cosmic Synthesis.

We are told that synthesis substands all existence. All diversities are preparations for future synthesis. All notes are in the process of building the Symphony of Cosmos.

Every thought that a man thinks, every word that a man speaks, every act that a man does either disturbs synthesis or builds toward it. If he is going toward synthesis he is on the right road. If he is going against synthesis, he is depriving himself of the greater joy, health, light and love of the future, and inviting toward himself forces of degeneration and decomposition.

Nature has its economy. Those elements that do not serve for synthesis are decomposed and used as fertilizers for future developments. Decomposition is the cycle of pain and suffering and the destruction of forms and civilizations and cultures.

One of the major causes of the extinction of races and nations is that they could not adapt themselves to the blueprint of synthesis. The defeat of a nation or a race starts from the moment it takes action against synthesis, or lives a life not in harmony with the currents of synthesis. The disappearance of races or nations takes a long time, but if one has eyes to see, he already notices the departure of the vitality and creativity of the race or nation.

Synthesis is sensed by those who develop intuition.

Synthesis echoes within all forms of life. This echo leads them to purposeful, goal-fitting living. Atoms, molecules and aggregations work toward synthesis. A tree, an animal, a man, a planet, a solar system, are travelers on the path of synthesis.

As synthesis is built within any living form, it develops greater power for survival.

Within the core of each living form the call of synthesis is heard. The lower kingdoms respond to the call of synthesis without resistance; but human beings, because of the development of I-consciousness and ego, reject, resist and even work against that call.

The mind does not synthesize; it separates. It is the heart that unites and leads toward synthesis. The first rays of intuition shine in the caves of the heart.

It is true that even the mind hears the call of synthesis, but its first reaction is to create ideologies, doctrines and groups that stand against each other in selfish, separative and aggressive attitudes. But the mind eventually traps itself within its own creation. After seeing the threat of its own creation, the mind tries to search for a way out. It is at this moment that the mind stretches itself toward the light of intuition.

The more light the mind receives from the intuition, the

more it works for synthesis, breaking the walls of the prisons in which it was enslaved through separative, selfish and egocentric actions.

Going against the currents of synthesis creates insanity, increase of crime and social disorders, and brings in depression and the collapse of governments and morals.

Nature as a whole is the result of right relationship between all Its parts. This is what the Cosmos means: a whole which is in harmony within itself.

Because of his power of thought man can create disturbances in the existence through his thoughts, speech and actions, bringing himself pain, suffering and confusion. The progress of man is a steady adjustment with Nature, with Its laws, principles and energies.

The success of man is to make himself a part of the synthesis of Cosmos and reduce and eliminate all that does not contribute to this synthesis.

Karma is the law which watches the process of synthesis and reacts to every motion taken against it, to reestablish equilibrium and synthesis.

Any **activity, ceremony** or creativity is the result of the cooperation of ideas, forces and visions. Any such conscious cooperation leads to synthesis, in which contrasting factors fade away and cooperating factors create the harmony of action.

Synthesis can only be achieved when the vision of the Common Good exists in the minds of those who are ready to cooperate with each other. The Common Good is the nucleus around which synthesis develops.

Disintegration takes place when the agents of integration no longer draw their inspiration from the nucleus.

This principle applies to culture. Culture flourishes and advances only if the core vision of creative persons is the Common Good, is the transformation and liberation of humanity. When the creative person uses his energies for his own personal interests, for his pleasures, or for his destructive purposes, he loses the core and his disintegration starts.

Every progressive and beneficial activity is based on cooperation and is aimed toward synthesis. Cooperation is the means through which all forces and energies are used harmoniously to produce synthesis.

Synthesis is a progressive unfoldment toward the future. The future exists only because of synthesis.

In the process of synthesis all elements of separatism gradually fall away and disappear. Man loses all those psychological or mental elements which keep him as a slave of his own self, of his own limitations; and he strives toward his greater Self which is inclusive and expanding.

In synthesis man expands in giving and becoming. In synthesis it is the vision of Beauty that controls all actions.

The process of synthesis is a process of absorption into beauty and into the vision of the good of all.

In synthesis man does not lose his individuality, as a color does not lose its individuality in a painting of a master artist. It is in becoming a harmonious part of the painting that his very existence of individuality is kept.

Each individuality is a note in the symphony of synthesis. They form a symphony because of the fact that in each of them the One Self is awakened and radiating.

Synthesis is the result of the awakening of the sense of Oneness.

When the One Self begins to awake in an individual he begins to contact, to relate and to communicate, in order to serve and to sacrifice. In reality, true sacrifice is a progressive actualization of synthesis, giving up all that is against the **whole**, and unfolding and developing all that is from and for the **whole**.

Real thought is a synthesis, and it develops toward greater synthesis. Analysis is a search for synthesis, if one does not lose the whole for the parts. Progressive thinking is a synthesizing process. In progressive thinking self-interest slowly disappears, and striving toward light increases. Everyone who thinks deeply and progressively is on the path of synthesis.

In the process of synthesis the heart plays the greatest role. It is by the inspiration and attractive power of the heart that things are related and brought into synthesis because the heart carries the flame of synthesis, the Self. The mind inspired by the heart becomes a great instrument of

11

synthesis and a servant of the Common Good.

Synthesis is achieved when the expanding Self finds response in our mental activities, or when certain mental activities evoke synthesis within the Self.

Each life form, each planet, each solar system and galaxy is a complete synthesis in its subjective side, where energies build a complete pattern or blueprint of highest synthesis. As this blueprint descends into manifestation layer after layer and is exposed to the various influences of the energies, forces, thoughts, emotions and disturbances of lower levels, much of the harmony of its parts is weakened or lost.

The forces of evolution try to restore the highest synthesis within the lowest manifestation and make it "as above, so below."

Each life form is consciously or unconsciously striving toward identifying with the prototype that originated the form. Like seeds, all life forms strive to bloom, or to be what their future is, hidden in the seed.

We may study the following tabulation:

Bodies	Initiation						
	1	2	3	4	5	6	7
physical	60	70	80	90	100	100	100
emotional	60	80	90	100	100	100	100
mental	60	80	90	100	100	100	100
Intuitional	10	20	50	75	100	100	100
Atmic	7	14	25	50	90	100	100
Monadic	5	10	20	50	80	90	100
Divine	2	5	10	25	50	75	100

The numbers in the squares above show how much each body is closer to the **prototype** (100). At each initiation the atomic substance increases in the bodies. Atomic substance is the highest level of each plane.

At the Seventh Initiation all bodies have reached perfection. Synthesis is achieved on seven levels of the Cosmic Physical Plane.

The numbers are not arithmetical, but a symbolic presentation of the process of synthesis. Synthesis is achieved on the Cosmic Physical Plane when the glory of the highest manifests through the lowest.

The increase of numbers at each initiation symbolizes also the increase of transformation in the vehicle itself. If it is 5, it means 5% transformation. If it is 100, it symbolizes total transformation into the prototype, or total synthesis.

The secret of health, prosperity and success is in the process of synchronization with the principle of synthesis in Nature.

Because of their attainment of synthesis, some individuals transmit powerful and magnetic energy wherever they are. If they are in a group, the group grows and flourishes. If they are in a city, they bring in a great amount of energy which can be used by those who are on the path of crime and by those who are on the path of holiness.

When our thoughts are in harmony with the principle of synthesis, we transmit a great amount of energy into our system and environment. Some people are magnets and sources of energy due to the fact that they stand and live for synthesis in their thoughts, words and actions.

This is why some very advanced individuals seek and live in solitude, not to stimulate the latent seeds of evil in the multitudes.

Every time a Great One appears, He takes a great risk because He knows that good as well as bad will be evoked from the people. A Great One prepares His disciples before He works with them more closely. He disciplines them with goodwill, right human relations, cooperation, service, gratitude, and makes them ready for synthesis. Every disciple of a Great One must think, speak and act in terms of synthesis to be worthy for higher guidance and sacrificial service.

It is absolutely true that when a man begins to think, to talk, to act and to live in the spirit of synthesis he transmits energy. This energy purifies him, uplifts him, inspires him, and heals him. Those who are receptive to his energy sense similar changes in their very nature.

One must realize that synthesis stands behind all diversities. Synthesis is the origin of all that exists and the ultimate goal of all that is.

The greatest honor that one can have is the achievement and realization of synthesis and the ability to hold synthesis and progressively advance into higher synthesis. The greatest failure of a man is to be trapped in the spirit of separatism. This is a great misery and calamity that can descend upon a person. Such a person is his own destroyer and enemy. All his actions eventually lead him into self-destruction.

Many beautiful seeds are destroyed before they open into fragrant flowers. Many nations perish before they perform their tasks...because the individual chose the path of isolation, because the nation followed a man or a group of men who taught separatism.

A separative synthesis is created when people unite into a group or a nation to destroy other groups and other nations. Separative synthesis is the most destructive force on this planet. We call such a synthesis aborted synthesis. Because of its separative nature in group form, the individuals of the group will have a very difficult time finding the path of true synthesis and thus delay their spiritual evolution.

When kings became totalitarian they were removed from their thrones. If so-called democratic governments turn to totalitarianism, they will again be removed from their chairs because life will never allow the process of synthesis to be hindered for a long period of time.

It is possible to eventually have a world government, but if the government turns to totalitarianism, it will be the greatest disaster for the progress of humanity, until humanity again washes away such obstacles on the path of synthesis.

Once we were in a forest and heavy rain began to fall. The river below us rose almost 15 feet. Watching the torrent of the river the Teacher said, "This is how synthesis works. Cyclically it carries away to the ocean all that hinders its path."

Totalitarianism is another form of failed synthesis. In true synthesis there is no imposition; there is development, unfoldment, transformation and spiritual magnetism. In a truly synthesized group, everyone knows his responsibility, and everyone does the best he can for the welfare of the whole group.

The leader in a group living in synthesis is only a reminder of synthesis or a spearhead for attainment of higher synthesis.

Any imposition creates failure in synthesis and eventually turns it into totalitarianism. Fanatics are the fruits of the totalitarian tree.

Totalitarianism is the most dangerous form of government because it drains a great amount of energy from the prototype which stands as the foundation of **Divine Totalitarianism**. Just as your whole system obeys your command, so it is going to be in the future for all creation: the Divine Will will rule the whole. But such a rule will be a synthesis, a common cooperation of parts with the whole, because the Divine Will is the will that will operate in each individual form as his own or Its own will. Thus the Divine Will will reveal Itself as one will manifesting through all that exists. Real free will is that stage of will when all have one will.

One day while I was walking with my Teacher in a meadow, he stopped and listened carefully to a big bell. Turning to me he said, "Did you hear that?"

"Yes, I did."

"It is cracked."

He hurried back to look at the big bell which was three feet high. When we came to the bell he hit it with his finger. Then he said to the watchman, "Take it down. I don't want to hear it."

"Sir, why? It is just a little cracked."

"No. It has no synthesis any more. We can't let cracked sound fill the Space."

Individual synthesis must proceed along the lines of collective synthesis. This is what history shows us.

If two people are separately synthesized they can form a nice synthesized family. If two million families are synthesized they can form a great nation. If all nations reach a degree of synthesis we will have a global master, one synthesized humanity. It is after such a synthesis that the Solar doors will open for us. But if each degree of synthesis creates a prison of separatism, it turns into an obstacle on the path of synthesis.

15

There is a very important point in the idea of synthesis: it is only possible to reach great heights of synthesis in group formation. Individual synthesis does not last until it lives in a group synthesis. It is in the group life that the essence of man is called forth, hindrances for synthesis are removed, and in test after test the disciple proves that he stands in synthesis.

It is, or course, possible to be a part of a subjective group and achieve great synthesis, and for a cycle of time not have any objective contact with objective groups on Earth, at least physically.

If any form on the mental, emotional or physical plane has no prototype, it does not bring joy, happiness and progress, and it becomes a burden. When one thinks and builds in harmony with the prototype it lasts; but if he builds on the patterns of his glamors, illusions, vanity and confusion, it does not last and brings unhappiness to the world.

There are groups and nations that do not embody a principle and they are not in the plan of the Leader of the Tower. Such groupings bring great suffering for humanity and also present a great test for humanity. But after a short while they disappear, though sometimes with heavy destruction. They are just like an artificial flower. They have no principle or life, no living prototype. It is true that man can build a prototype for it, but it soon dissolves. That is why all that is not built upon Beauty, Goodness, Truth and synthesis will not last long. The fire of the subtle world or the fire of the subterranean world will burn it.

Many civilizations were annihilated within the layers of the earth. Those forms which have prototypes remain, and when their time comes they pass to astral, mental and higher levels toward their essential prototype.

Synthesis is possible for elements which have principles or prototypes. Lies cannot create synthesis. It is impossible to create synthesis with ugliness, or beauty with chaos. Stealing and exploitation cannot be used for synthesis because they have no principle and they do not exist in the world of reality. To explain this further, we can say that the temple cannot be built by blocks of marble mixed with blocks of clay. A symphony cannot be composed on a piano which is out of tune.

Thus each idea, thought, and form must be purified and be a whole within itself, to be able to form a part in the Symphony.

One day the leader of our choir took a man out because his voice was flat. "You cannot sing because you don't have an ear," he said. "You cannot pick out and sing the pure note."

A company that works for its own interest eventually vanishes because self-interest has no true root. A company that works for the interests of humanity flourishes and expands because it has a living principle.

It is possible to be successful for a while, but all that you gather on the basis of selfish interest will eventually turn into a heavy taxation upon you because you misused the forces of Nature to create something unreal.

It is possible also to create great confusion in our system by thinking rightly but speaking and acting wrongly, or acting rightly with wrong motive. This is called in the Ancient Wisdom, building a structure upon the sand. It does not last long and falls, causing great damage for the owner.

The forces of darkness have no prototype in the Plan. Their activity has no principle or root, and all they intend to do will end in failure. But they have power and they use their power to prevent human beings from achieving synthesis and unity. They create lies and illusions and they try to prevent people from having subjective contact with the prototypal principles, so that they lose the path leading to synthesis.

If a person is on the path of synthesis they watch his every step. Any thought, word or action against synthesis gives them power upon him, and they use his every failure to take him away from the path of synthesis.

One cannot see synthesis until he is synthesized. The degree of synthesis reached within oneself will be the measure by which one can measure the expressions of synthesis going on around him.

Each instrument in the orchestra must be tuned in to itself and to the keynote of the orchestra. This is what health and synthesis are. Synthesis is harmony between the parts and the whole. Harmony is freedom. There is no freedom if there is no harmony. Freedom without harmony is madness or sickness.

17

No one can proclaim freedom if he is not related to anybody, to any nation or race. But in freedom he is in harmony with whatever he is related to. The more harmonious one is, the more free he is, and synthesis is freedom in harmony.

Synthesis is also economy. In synthesis there is no wastefulness. Every part of synthesis is goal-fitting. Energy and matter are distributed in the right proportion. Adaptability of the parts to the whole is economy.

All that is against synthesis wastes matter, energy, time and space, and brings pollution and depression. It is only in synthesis that waste is eliminated, greed is controlled and pollution is stopped.

Accuracy in construction is economy. Similarly, no synthesis can be achieved without accuracy and economy. Wastefulness cannot build synthesis. Synthesis is accuracy in matter, time, space and energy. Synthesis requires the highest dedication to the most essential. This is also done through right usage of all factors. Right usage is economy.

Synthesis works with two laws, the Law of Economy and the Law of Attraction. Man must learn the Law of Economy and demonstrate all Its aspects in his life. Then he must add to It the Law of Attraction, which is the ability to draw into his sphere all that will help him to achieve synthesis.

Economy organizes and purifies the personality. Attraction increases the love nature and establishes right relationship. The Law of Synthesis organizes the higher Cosmic ethers, or the higher spiritual bodies and centers, and relates the man with the Heart of Cosmos.

The point of synthesis is the moment of enlightenment, the moment of be-ness. The point of synthesis is the moment of deepest gratitude and purest humility.

Only on the path of the process of becoming your Self do you meet greater and greater values. The closer you go to your Self, the deeper you fuse with the One Self. Thus synthesis is arrived at through becoming the highest that you are essentially.

Synthesis must be achieved in all seven fields of human endeavor. In the political field humanity will eventually create a political synthesis which will be accepted by all people everywhere because it will meet the needs and the levels of all people on Earth. This synthesis will be built by the best and the highest that any political doctrine can contribute.

The same must be achieved in the educational field. An educational system must be created for the world as a whole.

Synthesis is not uniformity; it is an organism that can meet any need on any level without weakening its integrity and wholeness. In synthetic education the most essential principles will serve as integrating factors, but the methods and approaches will be adapted to any condition.

In the field of communication there is a process of synthesis going on, though at the present mostly for separative interests. The day will come when a synthesized communication will work for all humanity, everywhere.

In the field of art, great steps are being taken toward synthesis. But still we have few art objects which not only present national characteristics, but also global characteristics. Eventually global art is going to manifest, an art that is inspired by humanity and dedicated to humanity.

In the field of science great steps are being taken toward synthesis. But future synthesis will be far advanced and science will dedicate itself to meet human and global needs and strive into the unknown, into the far-off worlds; and also to investigate the invisible realms of human nature.

In the religious field great steps are being taken toward synthesis, but still separative walls stand erect as the symbols of human ignorance. Religious synthesis will be the dream of all religions, and it will unite all religions and compose a symphony in which there will be not only synthesis but also freedom for each religion and freedom for each man and woman in any religion.

Synthesis takes away complicating and disturbing aspects and emphasizes the harmonizing and strengthening aspects of religion, or of any field of human endeavor.

In the economic field synthesis will be unavoidable. It will bring prosperity and abundance to the world. Destructive competition will be put away and replaced by the golden rule of sharing. Great financiers will come and plan the blueprints of economic synthesis for one world.

19

When all these seven fields of human endeavor are separately synthesized, humanity will try to create a synthesis out of all these seven fields of human endeavor. This is how humanity will demonstrate its maturity and be ready to graduate from the planetary school.

Synthesis is a process and an achievement, but it is also the name of a powerful energy. Our machines cannot prove or discriminate this energy yet, but some subtle mechanism in the hearts of people senses this energy and uses it to further the process of synthesis in the whole world. Those who develop the sense of synthesis within their being gradually and increasingly dedicate their thoughts, words and actions to bring out synthesis in all fields of human endeavor.

We are told that there are two Avatars working at this time to bring synthesis and coordination. One of them is the Avatar of Synthesis, Who is working on the mental plane only. The other is the Avatar of Coordination, Who is working on the physical plane.

Coordination is an organizing, arranging, systematizing, relating and harmonizing process. The military, educational, financial and other fields are going through a coordination to be more effective and more economical.

Coordination on the physical plane and synthesis on the mental plane work together to bring synthesis within the three fields of human endeavor--physical, emotional and mental.

At this time not only is a great process of coordination going on on an international scale, but also an inner process of synthesis is evident in the thinking of humanity as a whole. Those who respond to the note of these great Avatars through their thinking and living establish a line of communication with Them, Who in certain cases overshadow them, inspire them, and cyclically come in contact with them to restore the great Plan and further the unfoldment of the Divine Purpose.

Overshadowing takes place when a disciple, through deep meditation and thinking, creates those thoughtforms which attract Their attention.

The Avataric force evokes the will aspect in the disciple and enthuses him to live a life of service and sacrifice for humanity.

Inspiration takes place when the disciple, standing as a soul, receives direct energy of inspiration from the Avatar, which reveals the tasks confronting him. The disciple, with full consciousness and willingness, cooperates with the inspiration received and dedicates his life to manifest the intention of the Avatar.

To receive inspiration and be overshadowed by the Avatar one must achieve purity of motive and purity of life; dedicate himself for the service of One humanity; and develop higher thinking and readiness to tune in with the Avataric force.

The third method by which Avatars contact humanity is direct manifestation. We are told that in the Age of Synthesis, or in the Aquarian Age, these three methods will be used more and more to create planetary and solar synthesis.

The great Teacher, D.K., speaking about the Avatar says that it is necessary to provide:

> "...a nucleus or group through which the Avatar of Synthesis can work when the lesser Avatar has come forth upon the mental plane. This involves individual activity, the sounding out of a clear note, based on clear mental perception, the recognition of those allied in the work and the development of conscious group work. In this group work the personality is subordinated and only the following determinations are dominant:
>
> a. The determination to offer group service -- as a group -- to the world group.
> b. The determination to establish right human relations upon the planet.
> c. The determination to develop everywhere the spirit of goodwill.
> d. The determination to withstand evil through planned group activity." [1]

1. Alice A. Bailey, *The Externalization of the Hierarchy*, p.312.

Synthesis is achieved by the power of psychic energy. As psychic energy increases, the power of synthesis develops further.

Psychic energy is the energy of the Central Cosmic Magnet. The magnet of the heart attracts this energy, which like a fiery stream releases the source of psychic energy sleeping in the heart.

Psychic energy links the head and throat centers and organizes them for the labor of synthesis. Psychic energy is attracted to the heart through unceasing striving toward perfection and mastery.

Christ is the flower of synthesis of milleniums. In Him all rays meet and burn as one flame. From Him radiates the pure psychic energy of the Sun. He nourishes with psychic energy all hearts that turn to Him. All dreams of perfection are synthesized in Him. He stands on the road of Infinity as a torch of synthesis. The glory of the Highest shines out of Him.

We are told that synthesis radiates an emerald flame. Immediately when this emerald flame is seen, the creative forces of Nature feel a pull of attraction toward the flame. The creativity of the flame of synthesis increases as the creative forces fuse with the flame. This is how synthesis opens the gates for Cosmic relationship.

Synthesis leads to happiness, joy and eventually to bliss. At the highest point of synthesis emanates an energy which is called bliss. Bliss is freedom, vitality, harmony and revelation.

Once a person tastes the moment of synthesis and its fragrance -- bliss, he will never rest until he consciously reaches the summit of synthesis and makes it a permanent place to communicate with Cosmic forces.

The highest point of synthesis is the magnet which polarizes all energies, cells and atoms of man and brings in them progressive harmonization and transformation. This highest point of synthesis is the Self, the Monad in man, which throughout centuries organizes the whole mechanism of the body, feelings and consciousness and makes them serve the purpose sensed and registered by the point of synthesis.

A similar process goes on throughout ages on the

planetary scale. The planet and all kingdoms in it have a point of synthesis from which emanates all those energies which create cooperation, synchronization and coordination, progressively building forms to serve holistic goals and eventually leading to synthesis. This point of synthesis is called by many names. It is called the Tower, or Shamballa, the Father's Home, or the Head Center of the planet. No matter what It is called, the history of humanity senses Its existence. It is an unseen magnet leading all atoms, all cells, and all individual forms of light to synthesis.

The progress of Nature clearly indicates the existence of such a Center.

As the seed of any life form eventually synthesizes to it highest point of manifestation; as the embryo becomes the man; as the acorn turns into a huge oak tree; similarly the purpose of the planet is achieved through progressive synthesis, to the culmination of highest synthesis. It is in this highest synthesis that the glory of life will manifest.

In the idea of synthesis we learn one very important lesson -- that all must be arranged and related in such a way that nothing is left out, but each form of life is included and related with its best aspects to produce the total synthesis. This process cannot be achieved by exclusion, or separativeness, by creating cleavages and segregations; but by unification, inclusiveness and fusion.

The most fundamental note or principle in Nature is synthesis.

If we study and analyze all moral, religious, and social rules and laws, we will find that all of them have one background, one axis: synthesis. Whatever is against synthesis or violates the future synthesis is a vice, is a crime. Whatever is for synthesis is a virtue, is a beneficent action, word or thought.

The future morality of groups and nations will be measured by the measure of synthesis. The greater is the synthesizing power of a nation, the greater is the vitality and radiation of a nation, and the longer is its lifespan.

This is also true for a man or for a woman. We will eventually learn that the most successful business, the most successful politics, the most successful spiritual life is based upon the idea of synthesis and directed to the goal of synthesis.

The thinking process of a man who is inspired by the idea of synthesis penetrates ages ahead and builds those bridges through which humanity passes in its most critical moments or needs. The giants of Spirit are those people who lived and labored in the light and purpose of synthesis.

Education in the New Age will be based upon the keynote of synthesis. Students will be challenged to think in terms of the whole, in relation to all that exists. They will be taught that all that they think, speak and do affects the whole. Responsibility is the realization of this idea.

It will be possible to prove scientifically that your thought affects your pen, your table, your clothes, your body, the trees, people everywhere...the stars. Once this holistic approach is grasped, it will be possible to raise world citizens, or even citizens of the universe.

The sense of responsibility is related to synthesis. No one can develop synthesis if he thinks that the world exists for himself alone. One day it will be proved that the absence of the process of synthesis in certain races was the cause of the extinction of those races. Under the whole construction of the education of the New Age will be the idea or the foundation of synthesis. All curricula, all true Teaching, will be based upon synthesis.

If we ignore the news presented to us by the world press, radio, and television, we will clearly see that in spite of all this negative news, fused with the spirit of fear, crime, destruction and despair, there exists a network of synthesis which is continuously and gradually paving the way of universal synthesis. Because of the noise of the news, people are not able to see this; but we have now fifty times more fusion, cooperation, coordination, relationship, holistic efforts and group striving than ten years ago. This is a great achievement about which the blind servants of greed never talk.

Observe how the system of communication is unifying the whole world. Observe how an increasing number of people are talking, dreaming, and working for one humanity.

See how more and more knowledge is available to

everyone. See how separatism is defeating itself. See how races are blending within each other.

All icy fragments of separatism will melt away as the sunshine of synthesis increases in its light and influence.

The forces of synthesis are proving the futility of all oppositions. This is the hope of glory for humanity. One day all those who built walls of separatism will deplore their acts and dedicate themselves to clear all consequences of their crimes.

Certain people build their rooms with bricks but do not use cement between them. Such buildings do not last because they lack the synthesizing factor. It is the vision of synthesis that holds things together.

A great building is the silent song of synthesis.

A great symphony is the glorification of synthesis.

A book or a lecture is great if it has the spirit of synthesis.

Human cultures and civilizations are the battlefields of two groups of forces:

    a.   those who fight to separate, to isolate, to exploit.

    b.   those who fight to include, to cooperate, and to synthesize.

In all walks of life synthesis is victorious. All human achievements in all fields of human endeavor are the result of synthesis. Radio, television, computers, and other sophisticated machinery sing the glory of synthesis of human thought.

All great transactions in business, in banking, in international marketing, are the victory of synthesis. One must see how the forces of separatism are already living the last moments of their lives.

Greater creative persons are those who have achieved the power of synthesis. They can even relate contradictory factors and make them reveal a vision. Actually, the creative process is entirely a process of synthesis.

As one proceeds on the path of synthesis, his integrity shines out. He becomes more productive, sacrificial and selfless. Selflessness is a great magnet which attracts all constructive forces and virtues for creative action.

In the future people will be measured by the measure of synthesis. A genius will create an electrical instrument which

25

will reveal the synthesis achieved in physical, emotional, mental and spiritual realms.

Many disciplines are given to humanity to lead it toward synthesis. The discipline of the Aquarian Age will be the discipline of fiery synthesis, a synthesis achieved with the fire of Spirit, fusing with the fires of Space.

The fires of Space are those rays or energies which relate and connect the man with the Cosmos, increasingly unfolding in him the sense of universality, wholeness and synthesis.

Once our Teacher said that all knowledge and sciences are related. Actually he said, "All sciences form a unified whole."

A student interrupted him and asked why all knowledge was related.

"Because," said the Teacher with a smile, "there is only one **Knower**. The parts of a machine can be a thousand, but in the mind of the Knower, there is only one synthesis, one machine." Pausing for a while he said in a whisper, "All things that exist are parts of one idea in the mind of the Knower."

A few days later when I saw the Teacher in the garden, I asked him, "Why did you whisper your thought in the class when answering our friend?"

He looked at me and said, "In the presence of sacred ideas I feel extremely humble."

Synthesis is the manifested purpose. It is synthesis that reveals the purpose, and it is the purpose that inspires meaning to every action.

Confusion is absence of synthesis. Certainty and stability are steps on the ladder of synthesis.

Beauty is a moment of synthesis. The greater is the synthesis, the greater and more unforgettable is the beauty. The more factors that are involved in synthesis, the greater is the beauty of the created form.

Creative geniuses are composers of the symphony of synthesis. In the future they will be called heroes of synthesis.

The science of synthesis needs millenniums to develop. Every living form is a witness of this long path. How many millions of years the Spirit strived to be a flower, to be a bird, to be a lion, to be a man...to be an angel. All these steps are steps of synthesis, and the human mind can understand synthesis as it experiences synthesis.

Self-satisfied people, people who run after their self-interests, often express great satisfaction with their achievements. They feel complete and perfect. Those who are on the path of synthesis continuously strive for greater synthesis. Every perfection or every success achieved by them becomes another stepping stone leading toward a more inclusive synthesis.

Self-satisfied people expect the world to be a leisure palace. But for those who seek synthesis, the world becomes a training school leading to synthesis.

The first ones are always disappointed in the moments of their highest satisfaction. For the second ones, the days are full of joy and surprises.

People sometimes think that psychic powers are the sign of greatness. This is true if the higher senses on higher planes are unfolded and synchronously function with the physical senses. But the highest attainment is the attainment of synthesis, when the Self or the Monad synthesizes in Itself all senses. Psychism disappears in the attainment of perfect synthesis because the perfected Self no longer needs any more instruments of contact.

To reach such an attainment man must not only pass through human initiation, but also planetary and solar initiations.

At the end of our journey in the Cosmic Physical Plane, we manifest the synthesis of Spirit. It is only through such a fiery synthesis that we will dare to enter into the Cosmic Astral Plane. We are told that nothing can resist dissolution on the astral plane but the power of synthesis.

After the earthly life, the achieved synthesis is like a shield that the Spirit puts on on the path toward the fiery spheres in Space. After one leaves the brain and body consciousness he needs a mechanism which instantaneously receives millions of impressions and synthesizes them into a decision or direction. Without such a mechanism the poor soul will fall into great confusion and uncertainty and run continuously after mirages. This is what happens in the astral world for those who lived a separative, selfish, fanatical life and closed their eyes and ears to the call of synthesis.

When a person exercises synthesis and develops the sense of synthesis in physical incarnation, he will easily find his way toward the higher worlds by orchestrating all various impressions and challenges into one symphony.

Creative labor and striving put the throat center into action. The throat center is called the instrument of synthesis. As this center unfolds and refines, the power of synthesis increases in man. But we are told that it is the heart that causes transformation of the throat center and enables it to function as the instrument of synthesis.

The center of synthesis is the heart. The whole Cosmos is reflected in the heart. It is this relationship between our heart and the Cosmic Heart that opens the gates of synthesis.

It is observed that some scientists are led by their own labor and discoveries, through their experiments, tests and machines. This is the halfway point of synthesis.

Gradually a new kind of scientist will emerge, who will have the gift of intuition and the ability to see beyond physical formations. He will have the eye of synthesis. He will compare his discoveries with the things that he sees on subtle levels, and he will eventually attain a knowledge characterized by synthesis.

No knowledge is safe and dependable if it is not put into action by the motive of synthesis. The tragedy of the discoveries and inventions of this epoch is that they are not aimed at bringing synthesis, but material interest or destruction.

The saddest thing in our life is when we lose an opportunity to uplift, to heal, to give, to enlighten or to synthesize. Such opportunities are called the diamond doors, which open for a short while and close when they feel the air of indifference and egotism.

The moments or days of opportunity are the moments and days in which you can transcend your level of beingness and consciousness. You can jump in the airplane carrying you to your life's destination...or you can miss the opportunity and stay in the darkness of your self-interest.

The challenge of the new age is synthesis. This is the door of opportunity for all humanity.

The future generations will open the pages of history, and they will either say, "Our ancestors missed the opportunity"; or "They were intelligent enough to stand in the spirit of synthesis and adorn the pages of history with their heroism. Peace be upon them."

The grandeur of Cosmos, the grandeur of the whole existence is gradually reflected in the soul of the man who carries in his Spirit the fire of synthesis.

PRACTICAL STEPS TO DEVELOP SYNTHESIS

1. Take 40 small blocks of wood and try to build different forms expressing different ideas.
2. Paint.
3. Compose music.
4. Organize an activity.
5. Take 20 words and form 20 sentences. Then try to form a small article with those 20 sentences.
6. Take opposite opinions or viewpoints and find lines of agreements within them, or create bridges between them.
7. Open a book and pick out a word and write an article about it.
8. Read about various religions as if you were born in each one of them, and then find a common denominator in them.
9. Take various objects and arrange them to express an idea.
10. Take five ideas and create one idea out of them.
11. Try to see what is:
    a. your ultimate goal in life.
    b. the most essential thing for humanity.
    c. something that belongs to the whole of humanity.
12. Take five objects and let them face five different directions. Find a way to make them "face the same direction" without moving them.

This will not be easy to do, but once you find the way to do it, new centers will become active in your mind.

13. Take some machines and disassemble them very carefully; then reassemble them. The more complicated is the mechanism, the better is the result.

14. Watch disputes and arguments; then in your own mind reach some conclusion or agreement between the two presentations.

15. Exercise tolerance, not as an escape or indifference but as a process of relationship and agreement.

16. Try to work under the pressure of a plan, or of a need, or of a purpose.

17. Carry on your chosen line of creative work under joy, pleasure or pain, suffering or distress. Let the idea or vision keep you going on.

18. Try to think about initiation in relation to:
    a. the individual
    b. the group, nation, and family
    c. humanity
    d. the globe
    e. the solar system
    f. the zodiac
    g. the galaxy

19. Think about a seed and in your visualization make it grow, flourish, bloom and radiate its glory. Do this very slowly, observing the harmonious development of its form, color and fragrance.

20. Cultivate compassion. Compassion is all-inclusive love and all-inclusive understanding.

21. Try to find a corresponding effect in the subjective world for each worldly action. Understand that all that is found in the objective world is found in the subjective world, too. Try to see the effect of your life on both of these worlds.

22. Think about yourself as existing in subjective and objective worlds simultaneously.

23. Let all your thoughts, words and actions be directed toward unity.

24. Try to see in all worldly events or objects the reflection of spiritual events and spiritual objects. See the meaning of "As above, so below."

25. When you talk to someone be aware that many invisible ones are listening to you, too. And when you think,

understand that your thoughts are resounding in the halls of the subjective world.

26. Try to see that you as a body and a spirit are part of the whole Existence. The only impossibility in Existence is that you cannot really separate yourself from the whole.

27. At every sunset send your love and blessings to all those whom the Sun will reach.

28. Try to think in the light of goodwill and right human relations. Try to make the idea of harmlessness the foundation of your thoughts.

Try to feel responsible for all your thoughts, words and deeds.

This is how you can change into a Son of Light, and in that Light see the purpose of your existence.

In the pure Teaching of the Spirit, the conscience is called the voice of synthesis.

Sedona, January 16, 1983.

WORKS BY TORKOM SARAYDARIAN

The Bhagavad Gita
The Science of Becoming Oneself
The Science of Meditation
The Psyche and Psychism
The Hierarchy and the Plan
Triangles of Fire
Five Great Mantrams of the New Age
The Legend of Shamballa
The Hidden Glory of the Inner Man
Christ, The Avatar of Sacrificial Love
Woman - Torch of the Future
Torchbearers
Irritation - The Destructive Fire
The Questioning Traveller and Karma
The Fiery Carriage and Drugs
The Spring of Prosperity
The Flame of Beauty, Culture, Love, Joy
Cosmos In Man
Dialogue With Christ
I Was
Symphony of the Zodiac
The Unusual Court(illustrated)